J $12.95
599.73   Wolpert, Tom
Wo   Whitetails

DATE DUE

FE 24 '92	JY 12 '04	
MR 9 '92	Y 26	
MR 28 '92		
JE 29 '92	AG 03	
SEP 21 9	G 15	
OCT 23 9	A 05	
AUG 05 9		
MR 04		
JA 17 '00		
FE 01 '0		
AP 23 0		
JY 06 04		

DEMCO

by Tom Wolpert

WHITETAILS

Whitetail Magic for Kids

Gareth Stevens Children's Books
MILWAUKEE

For a free color catalog describing Gareth Stevens' list of high-quality children's books, call 1-800-341-3569 (USA) or 1-800-461-9120 (Canada).

This North American edition published by
Gareth Stevens Children's Books
1555 North RiverCenter Drive, Suite 201
Milwaukee, Wisconsin 53212, USA

First published in 1990 by NorthWord Press, Inc., with a text by Tom Wolpert.
Copyright © 1990 by NorthWord Press, Inc.

Printed in the United States of America

1 2 3 4 5 6 7 8 9 97 96 95 94 93 92 91

Whitetail deer are the most common large game animals of North America. These deer get their name from their large tails. When frightened or alerted, their tails raise showing the white underfur as a warning signal to other whitetails.

Whitetail deer may stand as high as 3 feet and weigh up to 200 pounds. During spring and summer, whitetails have beautiful red coats which turn gray through fall and winter.

Whitetails have big brown eyes and narrow, graceful heads. Their lips grasp the vegetation on which they feed and their teeth are used for grinding and chewing.

SPRING

During late May and early June female whitetails, called does (dōze), look for a private place in the woods to be alone. Here they give birth to fawns - sometimes twin fawns!

Newborn fawns weigh from six to nine pounds. Although tiny and fragile, they can stand within 30 minutes of birth! Soon they are nursing on mother's milk - a milk high in protein and antibodies. These antibodies help protect fawns from disease during their first few weeks of life.

Does keep their fawns hidden from *predators* during the first month. Until strong, fawns may spend up to 12 hours a day snoozing and hiding. Fawns have *camouflage* coats to

help hide them in the woods. They do not run if a predator comes near. Instead, fawns lie quietly under cover not moving a muscle or blinking an eye.

By late spring, fawns are able to follow their mothers in search of food. While the fawns may nibble at fresh, new vegetation, they still depend on mother's milk. During these trips with mother, the fawns grow in strength and in knowledge of the world around them.

SUMMER

Summer in whitetail country is a lazy, peaceful time. Food is plentiful. The deer are eating tender grasses and weeds, shrubs, green leaves and farm crops. Whitetails have also been known to eat mushrooms, insects and even fish!

The growing fawns have a lot of time to play. Sometimes they run circles around their mothers. They jump and kick their hind legs and chase one another. This playing helps the fawns strengthen muscles and improve coordination.

The fawns are also learning deer behavior by watching their mothers and other deer. For example, after watching a buck challenge another deer, a fawn often attempts to challenge another fawn. This is called "learning by imitation".

AUTUMN

During autumn fawns begin to reach their full growth. It is also an important period when fawns and all deer must build up fat for the coming winter.

Whitetails now search for high energy foods like acorns, beechnuts, apples, cherries, grapes and other fruits. They especially like farm crops like corn, soybeans, milo and rye.

Since summer the male whitetails, called bucks, have been growing antlers. At first these antlers were very small, soft and tender. A thin, fuzzy skin called velvet covered them. This velvet dries up during autumn when the antlers reach their full growth. Then the bucks rub their hard antlers against trees and bushes to scrape off the old velvet.

Now the breeding season has begun. Strong, healthy bucks with big antlers breed most of the does. Bucks often fight one another by locking antlers. They push back and forth until the weaker buck is chased away. Then the strong buck goes off with a doe to breed. This begins the cycle for a new fawn in the spring.

WINTER

Winter in whitetail country, especially in the north, can be a very dangerous time for deer. Deep snow makes travel through the woods difficult. Freezing temperatures and winds continue for months.

Fortunately, whitetails *adapt* very well to cold weather. Their coats are made up of hollow hairs. Snow and wind cannot penetrate these hairs to the skin, so deer keep dry and warm.

Also, before the snow becomes too deep the whitetails have travelled as far as a mile from their resting sites to feed. By doing this they save nearby food for times when snow becomes too deep.

In winter there is not a lot of food available. Deer must eat bark, buds, twigs and even needles of certain trees. They also use their *hooves* to dig through snow to find nuts and acorns.

During long, hard winters many fawns may die. This is because they are small and do not have enough body fat to sustain them. Seventy percent of the deer that die in winter are fawns.

All whitetails, but especially fawns, may be attacked and killed by predators during the winter. Timber wolves, mountain lions, coyotes, bobcats and even house dogs will kill and eat deer. Many of the deer killed are small or weak. Usually these deer would not have survived the winter anyway.

Finally, the snows begin to melt and the new growth of spring appears. By this time the surviving fawns have lost 30 percent of their weight. All deer feed hungrily in the warm woods and meadows.

Now the cycle begins again in whitetail country. The fawns are now called "yearlings". They have learned many lessons of survival. The mother does will soon leave them to give birth to new fawns.

Some day the yearlings will become mature does or bucks and
guide their fawns through the seasons . . .
the seasons of the whitetail.

GLOSSARY

The words below also appear in the text in *italicized* type. The page number on which each word first appears is listed after each definition.

Adapt: To adjust or conform to a certain way of living (page 35).

Camouflage: A coloring disguise that hides an object from view (page 14).

Hooves: Curved coverings of horn that protect feet (page 39).

Predators: Animals that eat other animals to survive (page 14).

ADULT-CHILD INTERACTION QUESTIONS

These are questions you may ask young readers to get them to think about whitetails as viable occupants of a niche in the food chain. Encourage them to explain their feelings about whitetails and to ask their own questions. Clarify any misunderstandings they may have about the predator-prey relationship as it relates to deer, and explain the need to have predators and prey in the world. In this way, you can help foster future generations of environmentally aware and appreciative adults.

1. Have you ever seen a deer? If so, where? If not, where do you think you would be most likely to see one?

2. Newborn fawns can stand up within thirty minutes of birth. Human babies can take more than a year to stand and walk. Why do you think there is such a difference?

3. Why do you think fawns lie very still when a predator is near, instead of running away?

4. Why do you think the coats of whitetails turn from red to brown in fall and winter?

5. Fawns learn proper behavior by imitating other deer. Do human children do this? If so, how?

6. Why is it important for deer to build up fat during the spring and summer?

7. What good are antlers to male deer? Why don't female deer have them?

8. What is it that enables the deer to stay warm and dry during the winter?

9. Why do so many fawns fall prey to predators during the winter?

10. How do you think it feels to be a fawn?